לֶךְ לְךָ

The Journey of Abraham and Sarah

לֶךְ לְךָ

The Journey of Abraham and Sarah

Adapted by
Alison Greengard

Illustrated by
Carol Racklin-Siegel

EXCERPTED FROM
THE BOOK OF GENESIS

EKS Publishing Co., Oakland, California

In memory of my father,
Bernard Bernstein.
—Alison

For my son, Daniel.
—Carol

Adapted by Alison Greengard

Illustrated by Carol Racklin-Siegel

Edited by Jessica Goldstein

Book Design by Irene Imfeld

Composition by Archetype Typography

Abraham and Sarah ©2004 by EKS Publishing Co. Printed in Canada. No part of this book may be transmitted or reproduced by any means, electronic or mechanical, without written permission, except for brief quotations included in critical articles and reviews. For information, contact the publisher.

EKS Publishing Co.
P.O. Box 9750 Berkeley, CA 94709-0750
email: orders@ekspublishing.com
Phone (510) 251-9100 Fax (510) 251-9102
www.ekspublishing.com

First Printing July, 2004
ISBN 0-939144-49-2

Introduction

The *Journey of Abraham and Sarah* continues the EKS Publishing series of Bible stories for young readers. Stories about Abraham and Sarah appear in Genesis 12-25. For this version of the story, we have focused on Abraham and Sarah's journey to Canaan, their righteousness, and the surprising birth of their son Isaac.

In telling this story, we have necessarily omitted many sentences and shortened others, but we have not changed or added any text. Each page offers a meaningful—but not always literal—translation. For readers studying Hebrew, we have included a literal translation at the end of the story. A glossary at the back of the book gives the meaning and pronunciation of each word in *Abraham and Sarah*. The glossary lists words exactly as they appear in the story.

Readers may immediately notice that the Hebrew title, *Lech Lecha* or "Go out" does not match the English title, *The Journey of Abraham and Sarah*. This mismatch is no accident—instead it reflects two different traditions for titling stories. Many ancient works do not have titles or have titles that are unknown to us. To compensate, modern and ancient scholars regularly refer to these works by citing the first word or words in them. *Lech Lecha* is actually the title of a weekly Torah reading, or *parasha*. The story, as we present it, spans two readings, and we have thus given it an English subtitle that references the content of the story rather than the parasha of *Lech Lecha*.

Names are an important element in Biblical narratives. Name changes, bestowed in the Bible by God, usually occur when a character is confronting transformation. Sarah and Abraham are on both a physical journey as they travel to Canaan, and a spiritual one, as they begin to acknowledge God's presence and power. Thus, when *Abram*, meaning "the father is exalted," learns of his destiny as the Patriarch of the Jewish people, his name is expanded to *Abraham*. The names *Sarai* and *Sarah* probably both mean "princess," and her name change signifies her new and unexpected role as a mother. Genesis itself explains how Isaac got his name. Coming at a time when Abraham and Sarah were, by their own reckoning, far too old to have children, Isaac's name derives from the Hebrew word for laughter and highlights the joyous surprise of his arrival.

We hope that readers of all ages will enjoy the story of Abraham and Sarah and come to appreciate the language and beauty of the Hebrew Bible.

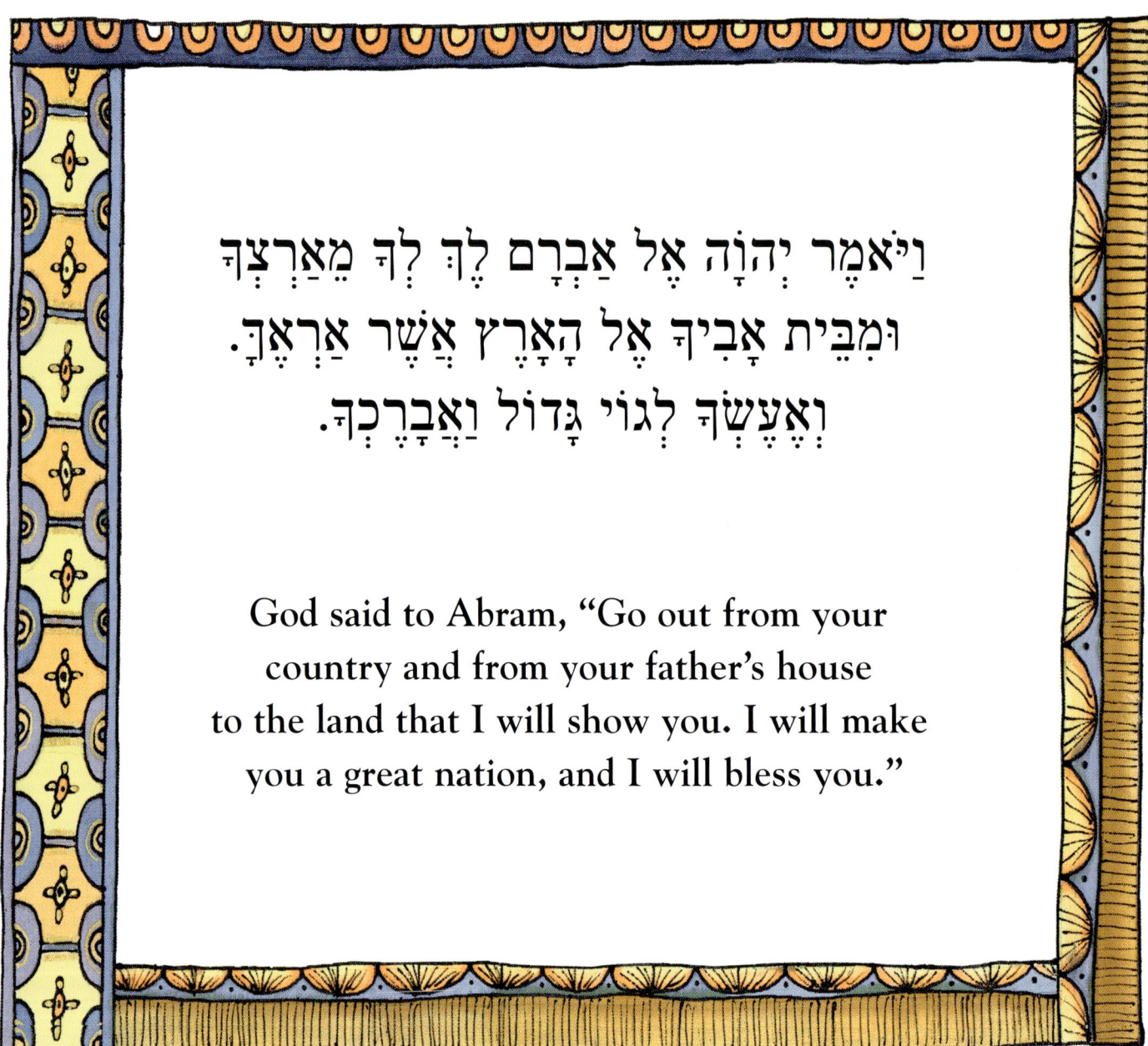

וַיֹּאמֶר יְהֹוָה אֶל אַבְרָם לֶךְ לְךָ מֵאַרְצְךָ
וּמִבֵּית אָבִיךָ אֶל הָאָרֶץ אֲשֶׁר אַרְאֶךָּ.
וְאֶעֶשְׂךָ לְגוֹי גָּדוֹל וַאֲבָרֶכְךָ.

God said to Abram, "Go out from your country and from your father's house to the land that I will show you. I will make you a great nation, and I will bless you."

וַיֵּלֶךְ אַבְרָם כַּאֲשֶׁר דִּבֶּר אֵלָיו יְהוָה.
וַיִּקַּח אֶת שָׂרַי אִשְׁתּוֹ
וַיֵּצְאוּ לָלֶכֶת אַרְצָה כְּנַעַן.

So Abram went, as the Lord had commanded him.
He took his wife Sarai with him, and they
set out for the land of Canaan.

הָיָה דְבַר יְהֹוָה אֶל אַבְרָם בַּמַּחֲזֶה. וַיּוֹצֵא אֹתוֹ הַחוּצָה וַיֹּאמֶר הַבֶּט נָא הַשָּׁמַיְמָה וּסְפֹר הַכּוֹכָבִים אִם תּוּכַל לִסְפֹּר אֹתָם. וַיֹּאמֶר לוֹ כֹּה יִהְיֶה זַרְעֶךָ.

The word of God came to Abram in a dream.
God took him outside and said, "Look
up at heaven and count the stars,
if you can count them all. That's how many
children and grandchildren you will have."

וַיֹּאמֶר לְאַבְרָם יָדֹעַ תֵּדַע כִּי גֵר יִהְיֶה זַרְעֲךָ בְּאֶרֶץ לֹא לָהֶם וַעֲבָדוּם וְעִנּוּ אֹתָם אַרְבַּע מֵאוֹת שָׁנָה. יָשׁוּבוּ הֵנָּה. לְזַרְעֲךָ נָתַתִּי אֶת הָאָרֶץ הַזֹּאת.

God said, "Know that your children will be strangers in a land and they will be slaves there for four hundred years. But they will return here, and I will give this land to them."

וְשָׂרַי לֹא יָלְדָה לוֹ. וַיְהִי אַבְרָם בֶּן תִּשְׁעִים שָׁנָה וְתֵשַׁע שָׁנִים. וַיֵּרָא יְהֹוָה אֶל אַבְרָם וַיֹּאמֶר אֵלָיו וְלֹא יִקָּרֵא עוֹד אֶת שִׁמְךָ אַבְרָם וְהָיָה שִׁמְךָ אַבְרָהָם. וְנָתַתִּי לְךָ וּלְזַרְעֲךָ אֵת כָּל אֶרֶץ כְּנָעַן.

Now Sarai had no children. And when Abram was ninety-nine years old, God appeared to him and said, "You will no longer be called Abram. Your name is now Abraham. And I will give to you and your children all the land of Canaan."

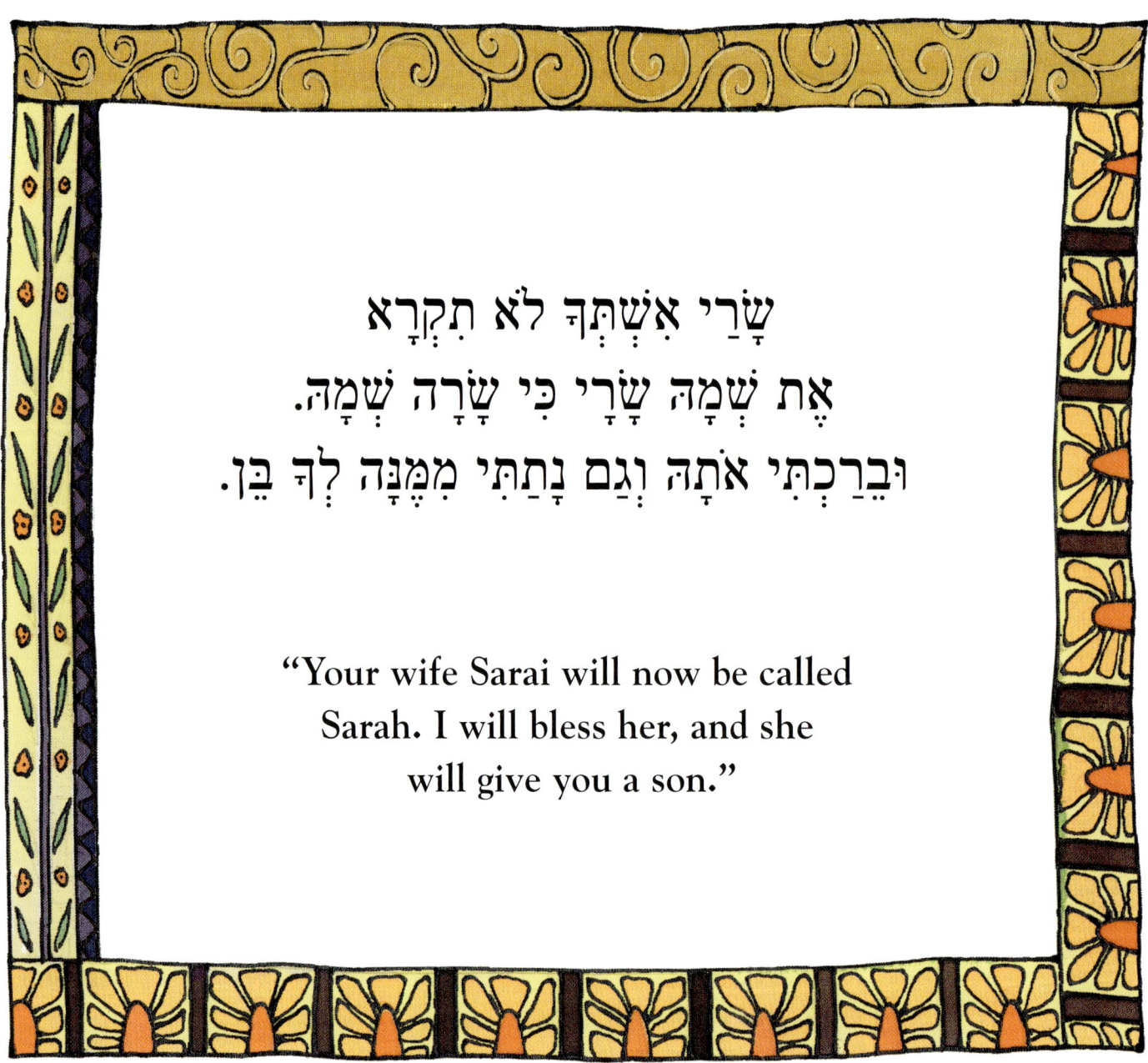

שָׂרַי אִשְׁתְּךָ לֹא תִקְרָא
אֶת שְׁמָהּ שָׂרָי כִּי שָׂרָה שְׁמָהּ.
וּבֵרַכְתִּי אֹתָהּ וְגַם נָתַתִּי מִמֶּנָּה לְךָ בֵּן.

"Your wife Sarai will now be called Sarah. I will bless her, and she will give you a son."

וְהוּא יֹשֵׁב פֶּתַח הָאֹהֶל וְהִנֵּה שְׁלֹשָׁה אֲנָשִׁים נִצָּבִים עָלָיו. וַיָּרָץ לִקְרָאתָם. וַיִּקַּח חֶמְאָה וְחָלָב וּבֶן הַבָּקָר וַיִּתֵּן לִפְנֵיהֶם וַיֹּאכֵלוּ.

One day, Abraham was sitting by the door of his tent when he saw three men standing before him. He ran to greet them, and he set food out for them, and they ate.

וַיֹּאמְרוּ אֵלָיו אַיֵּה שָׂרָה וַיֹּאמֶר הִנֵּה בָאֹהֶל. וַיֹּאמֶר שׁוֹב אָשׁוּב אֵלֶיךָ כָּעֵת חַיָּה וְהִנֵּה בֵן לְשָׂרָה אִשְׁתֶּךָ. וְשָׂרָה שֹׁמַעַת וַתִּצְחָק.

The men asked, "Where is Sarah?" and Abraham replied, "In the tent." One of the men said, "I will return next spring, and your wife Sarah will have a son by then." Sarah was listening to them, and she laughed.

וַיהוָה פָּקַד אֶת שָׂרָה כַּאֲשֶׁר אָמָר וַתֵּלֶד שָׂרָה בֵּן. וַיִּקְרָא אַבְרָהָם אֶת שֶׁם בְּנוֹ יִצְחָק. וַתֹּאמֶר שָׂרָה צְחֹק עָשָׂה לִי אֱלֹהִים.

God remembered Sarah as he promised, and Sarah had a son. Abraham called his son Isaac, and Sarah said, "God has brought me laughter."

Literal Translation

The Lord said to Abram, "Go out from your homeland and from your father's house, to the land that I will show you." I will make you a great nation, and I will bless you.

So Abram went as the Lord had commanded him. He took his wife Sarai, and they set out for the land of Canaan.

The word of the Lord came to Abram in a vision. He [God] took him [Abram] outside and said," Look toward heaven and count the stars, if you are able to count them." He [God] said to him [Abram], "So shall your descendants be."

He [God] said to Abram, "Know that your descendants shall be strangers in a land that is not theirs, and they shall be enslaved and oppressed for four hundred years. But they shall come back here. I grant this land to your descendants."

Sarah had not borne him [Abram] any children. When Abram was ninety-nine years old, the Lord appeared to Abram and said to him, "You will no longer be called Abram, but your name will now be Abraham. I will give to you and your descendants all the land of Canaan.

"Sarai your wife, will now be called Sarah. I will bless her and I will give you a son by her."

He [Abraham] was sitting at the door of his tent, and behold, three men stood before him. He ran to greet them. He took curds and milk and a calf, and he set it before them, and they ate.

They said to him, "Where is Sarah?" And he said, "In the tent." He [one of the men] said, I will return to you in the spring, and behold your wife Sarah will have a son." Sarah was listening, and she laughed.

The Lord remembered Sarah as he promised, and Sarah bore a son. Abraham called his son Isaac. And Sarah said, "God has brought me laughter."

Glossary

א

אָבִיךָ	a-**vee**-cha	your father
אַבְרָהָם	av-ra-**ham**	Abraham
אַבְרָם	av-**ram**	Abram
אַיֵּה	ay-**yay**	where
אֶל	**el**	to
אֱלֹהִים	e-lo-**heem**	God
אֵלָיו	ay-**lav**	to him
אֵלֶיךָ	ay-**le**-cha	to you
אִם	**eem**	if
אָמַר	a-**mar**	he said
אֲנָשִׁים	a-na-**sheem**	men
אַרְאֶךָּ	ar-**e**-cha	I will show you
אַרְבַּע	ar-**ba**	four
אֶרֶץ	**e**-rets	land
אַרְצָה	ar-**tsa**	to the land
אָשׁוּב	a-**shoov**	I will return
אֲשֶׁר	a-**sher**	that
אִשְׁתּוֹ	eesh-**to**	his wife
אִשְׁתְּךָ/אִשְׁתֶּךָ	**eesh**-te-cha	your wife
אֶת/אֵת	**et/ayt**	not translatable
אֹתָהּ	o-**ta**	her

אֹתוֹ	o-**to**	him
אֹתָם	o-**tam**	you (plural)

ב

בָּאֹהֶל	va-**o**-hel	in the tent
בְּאֶרֶץ	be-**e**-rets	in a land
בַּמַּחֲזֶה	ba-ma-cha-**ze**	in a vision
בֵּן/בֶּן	**vayn/bayn**	son
בֶּן תִּשְׁעִים שָׁנָה וְתֵשַׁע שָׁנִים	**ben** teesh-**eem** sha-**na** ve-**tay**-sha sha-**neem**	was ninety-nine years old
בְּנוֹ	be-**no**	his son

ג

גָּדוֹל	ga-**dol**	big
גֵּר	**gayr**	stranger

ד

דְּבַר	de-**var**	the word
דִּבֶּר	deeb-**ber**	he commanded

ה

הָאֹהֶל	ha-**o**-hel	the tent
הָאָרֶץ	ha-**a**-rets	the land
הָאָרֶץ הַזֹּאת	ha-**a**-rets ha-**zot**	this land
הַבֵּט	ha-**bet**	look!
הַחוּצָה	ha-**choo**-tsa	outside

הָיָה	ha-**ya**	was
הַכּוֹכָבִים	ha-**co**-cha-**veem**	the stars
הִנֵּה	hee-**nay**	behold
הֵנָּה	**hay**-na	here
הַשָּׁמַיְמָה	ha-sha-**mai**-ma	to the heavens

ו

וַאֲבָרֶכְךָ	va-a-va-**rech**-cha	I will bless you
וְאֶעֶשְׂךָ	ve-e-es-**cha**	I will make you
וּבֶן הַבָּקָר	oo-**ven** ha-ba-**kar**	and the calf
וּבֵרַכְתִּי	oo-**vay**-rach-tee	I will bless
וְגַם	ve-**gam**	and also
וְהוּא	ve-**hoo**	and he
וְהָיָה	ve-ha-**ya**	and will be
וְהִנֵּה	ve-hee-**nay**	behold
וְחָלָב	ve-cha-**lav**	and milk
וַיֹּאכְלוּ	va-yo-**chay**-loo	they ate
וַיֹּאמֶר	va-**yo**-mer	he said
וַיֹּאמְרוּ	va-yo-me-**roo**	they said
וַיהוָה	va-a-do-**nai**	and the Lord
וַיְהִי	vai-**hee**	he was
וַיּוֹצֵא	va-yo-**tsay**	he went out
וַיֵּלֶךְ	va-**yay**-lech	he went
וַיֵּצְאוּ	va-**yayts**-oo	they went
וַיִּקַּח	va-yee-**kach**	he took

וַיִּקְרָא	va-yeek-**ra**	he called
וַיַּרְא	va-**yay**-ra	he saw
וַיָּרָץ	va-ya-**rats**	he ran
וַיִּתֵּן	va-yee-**tayn**	he gave
וְלֹא	ve-**lo**	no
וּלְזַרְעֲךָ	oo-le-zar-**a**-cha	to your descendants
וּמִבֵּית	oo-mee-**bayt**	from the house of
וְנָתַתִּי	ve-na-**ta**-tee	I will give
וּסְפֹר	oo-se-**por**	and count
וַעֲבָדוּם	va-a-va-**doom**	they shall be enslaved
וְעִנּוּ	ve-ee-**noo**	they shall serve
וְשָׂרָה	ve-sa-**ra**	and Sarah
וְשָׂרַי	ve-sa-**rai**	and Sarai
וַתֹּאמֶר	va-**to**-mer	she said
וַתֵּלֶד	va-**tay**-led	she gave birth to
וַתִּצְחַק	va-teets-**chak**	she laughed
וְתֵשַׁע	ve-**tay**-sha	and nine

ז

זַרְעֲךָ	zar-**e**-cha	your descendants

ח

חַיָּה	chay-**ya**	reviving
חֶמְאָה	chem-**a**	curds

י

יֵדַע תֵּדַע	ya-**do**-a tay-**da**	you will know
יְהוָה	a-do-**nai**	the Lord
יִהְיֶה	yeeh-**ye**	will be
יָלְדָה	yal-**da**	given birth
יִצְחָק	yeets-**chak**	Isaac
יִקָּרֵא	yeek-ka-**ray**	will be called
יָשַׁב	yo-**shayv**	sat
יָשׁוּבוּ	ya-**shoov**-oo	they will return

כ

כַּאֲשֶׁר	ka-a-**sher**	as
כֹּה	**ko**	so
כִּי	**kee**	that, because
כָּל	**kol**	all
כְּנַעַן	ke-**na**-an	Canaan
כָּעֵת	ka-**ayt**	the season

ל

לֹא	**lo**	not, no
לְאַבְרָם	le-av-**ram**	to Abram
לְגוֹי	le-**goy**	a nation
לָהֶם	la-**hem**	theirs
לוֹ	**lo**	to him

לְזַרְעֲךָ	le-zar-**a**-cha	to your descendants
לִי	**lee**	for me
לְךָ	le-**cha**	you/to you
לֵךְ	**lech**	go!
לָלֶכֶת	la-**le**-chet	to go
לִסְפֹּר	lees-**por**	to count
לִפְנֵיהֶם	leef-nay-**hem**	before them
לִקְרָאתָם	leek-ra-**tam**	to greet them
לְשָׂרָה	le-sa-**ra**	to Sarah

מ

מֵאוֹת	may-**ot**	hundreds
מֵאַרְצְךָ	may-**ar**-tse-cha	from your land
מִמֶּנָּה	meem-**me**-na	from her

נ

נָא	**na**	please
נִצָּבִים	neets-tsa-**veem**	were standing
נָתַתִּי	na-**ta**-tee	I will give

ע

עוֹד	**od**	still/again
עָלָיו	a-**lav**	on (in front of) him
עָשָׂה	a-**sa**	he made

פ

פָּקַד	pa-**kad**	he remembered/visited
פֶּתַח	**pe**-tach	opening

צ

צְחֹק	tse-**chok**	laughter

שׁ

שׁוֹב	**shov**	again
שְׁלֹשָׁה	she-lo-**sha**	three
שֵׁם	**shem**	name
שְׁמָהּ	she-**ma**	her name
שִׁמְךָ	sheem-**cha**	your name
שֹׁמַעַת	sho-**ma**-at	she listened
שָׁנָה	sha-**na**	year
שָׁנִים	sha-**neem**	years

שׂ

שָׂרָה	sa-**ra**	Sarah
שָׂרַי	sa-**rai**	Sarai

ת

תֵּדַע	tay-**da**	you will know
תּוּכַל	too-**chal**	you can
תִּקְרָא	teek-**ra**	she will be called
תִּשְׁעִים	teesh-**eem**	ninety